MORE THAN A BUSINESS

'We decided it was time to end the almost customary half-hearted manner in which cheap editions were produced – as though the only people who could possibly want cheap editions must belong to a lower order of intelligence. We, however, believed in the existence in this country of a vast reading public for intelligent books at a low price, and staked everything on it'
Sir Allen Lane, 1902–1970

'The Penguin Books are splendid value for sixpence, so splendid that if other publishers had any sense they would combine against them and suppress them'
George Orwell

'More than a business ... a national cultural asset'
Guardian

'When you look at the whole Penguin achievement you know that it constitutes, in action, one of the more democratic successes of our recent social history'
Richard Hoggart

Lady Chatterley's Trial

EDITED BY C. H. ROLPH

PENGUIN BOOKS

PENGUIN BOOKS

Published by the Penguin Group

Penguin Books Ltd, 80 Strand, London WC2R ORL, England

Penguin Group (USA) Inc., 375 Hudson Street, New York, New York 10014, USA

Penguin Group (Canada), 10 Alcorn Avenue, Toronto, Ontario, Canada M4V 3B2
(a division of Pearson Penguin Canada Inc.)

Penguin Ireland, 25 St Stephen's Green, Dublin 2, Ireland
(a division of Penguin Books Ltd)

Penguin Group (Australia), 250 Camberwell Road, Camberwell, Victoria 3124,
Australia (a division of Pearson Australia Group Pty Ltd)

Penguin Books India Pvt Ltd, 11 Community Centre,
Panchsheel Park, New Delhi – 110 017, India

Penguin Group (NZ), cnr Airborne and Rosedale Roads, Albany,
Auckland 1310, New Zealand (a division of Pearson New Zealand Ltd)

Penguin Books (South Africa) (Pty) Ltd, 24 Sturdee Avenue,
Rosebank 2196, South Africa

Penguin Books Ltd, Registered Offices: 80 Strand, London WC2R ORL, England

www.penguin.com

The Trial of Lady Chatterley first published in Penguin Books 1961
This extract published as a Pocket Penguin 2005

1

Copyright © Penguin Books, 1961
All rights reserved

Set in 11/13pt Monotype Dante
Typeset by Palimpsest Book Production Limited
Polmont, Stirlingshire
Printed in England by Clays Ltd, St Ives plc

Contents

Regina v. Penguin Books Ltd
October 1960, Old Bailey

The following extracts from the trial, drawn from C. H. Rolph's classic *The Trial of Lady Chatterley*, are designed simply to give a flavour of the proceedings rather than pursue all the trial's ins and outs, and it is hoped that it is reasonably fair to both sides.

The Opening Address for the Prosecution

Mervyn Griffith-Jones

'If your Lordship pleases. Members of the Jury, I appear with my learned friend Mr Morton to prosecute in this case. The defendant company, Penguin Books Limited, is represented by my learned friends Mr Gerald Gardiner, Mr Jeremy Hutchinson, and Mr Richard du Cann.

'This company, as you have just heard, is charged with publishing an obscene article which is, in effect, the book *Lady Chatterley's Lover*, written by D. H. Lawrence some time about 1928 and now published, or proposed to be published, for the first time in this country.

'Members of the Jury, Penguin Books Limited need no introduction to you. They are the well-known and, let me say at once, highly reputable firm of publishers incorporated in 1936 and publishing Penguin Books. It was learnt earlier this year that that company proposed to publish this book, *Lady Chatterley's Lover*. As a result of that the company were seen in August by the police, and as a result of the conversations which took place it was arranged that prior to the actual release of this book, which at that time was planned for 25 August, the company should, in effect, provide evidence of a publication of the book in order that it should be brought before a jury really as a test case, so far as a criminal case can be a test case, in order to obtain a verdict from a jury as to whether or not this book was an obscene book within the meaning of the law. And so it comes about that you are now in that jury box to give your verdict upon this book, *Lady Chatterley's Lover*.

'Let me emphasize it on behalf of the Prosecution: do not approach this matter in any priggish, high-minded, super-correct, mid-Victorian manner. Look at it as we all of us, I hope, look at things today, and then, to go back and requote the words of Mr Justice Devlin, "You will have to say, is this book to be tolerated or not?", in the sense that it must tend, or may tend, to deprave and corrupt. Members of the Jury, when you have seen this book, making all such allowances in favour of it as you can, the Prosecution will invite you to say that it does tend, certainly that it may tend, to induce lustful thoughts in the minds of those who read it. It goes further, you may think. It sets upon a pedestal promiscuous and adulterous intercourse. It commends, and indeed it sets out to commend, sensuality almost as a virtue. It encourages, and indeed even advocates, coarseness and vulgarity of thought and of language. You may think that it must tend to deprave the minds certainly of some and you may think many of the persons who are likely to buy it at the price of 3s. 6d. and read it, with 200,000 copies already printed and ready for release.

3

'You may think that one of the ways in which you can test this book, and test it from the most liberal outlook, is to ask yourselves the question, when you have read it through, would you approve of your young sons, young daughters – because girls can read as well as boys – reading this book. Is it a book that you would have lying around in your own house? Is it a book that you would even wish your wife or your servants to read?

'Let me at once – because not for one moment do I wish to overstate this case – let me at once concede that D. H. Lawrence is a well-recognized and indeed great writer. Let me at once concede, but perhaps not to so great an extent, that there may be some literary merit in this book. I put it no higher. Certainly let me concede that some of his books have great literary merit. All that I concede. But, again, you have – have you not? – to judge this book, balancing the extent of the obscenity (if you so find it is obscene) against any interests of literature, art and so on, and you have to say in the end, balancing the whole thing, the one against the other: is its publication proved to be justified for the public good?

'And so we come, members of the Jury, to the book itself. And you must forgive me if I have occupied too much of your time in preliminaries. The book has been passed to you. It is a book about – if I may summarize it in literally a word almost – Lady Chatterley, who is a young woman whose husband was wounded in the First World War. They were married at the beginning of the war; he comes back wounded so that he is crippled and paralysed from the waist downwards and unable to have any sexual intercourse. Members of the Jury, other views may be put before you; I invite you to say that, in effect, the book is a book describing how that woman, deprived of sex from her husband, satisfies her sexual desires – a sex-starved girl – how she satisfies that starvation with a particularly sensual man who happens to be her husband's gamekeeper. And you have the episodes of sexual intercourse. There are, I think, described in all thirteen throughout the course of this book. You will see that they are described in the greatest detail, save perhaps for the first. You may think that this book, if its descriptions had been confined to the first occasion on which sexual intercourse is described, would be a very much better book than it is. But twelve of them certainly are described in detail leaving nothing to the imagination. The curtain is never drawn. One follows them not only into the bedroom but into bed and one remains with them there.

'Members of the Jury, that is not strictly accurate, because the only variations, in effect, between all thirteen occasions are the time and the *locus in quo*, the place where it happened. So one does not follow them into the bed and remain with them in bed; one starts in my lady's boudoir, in her husband's house, one goes to the floor of a hut in the forest with a blanket laid down as a bed; we see them do it again in the undergrowth in the forest amongst the shrubbery, and not only in the undergrowth in the forest, in the pouring rain, both of them stark naked and dripping with raindrops. One sees them in the keeper's cottage, first in the evening on the hearth rug and then we have to wait until dawn to see them do it again in bed. And finally, members of the Jury, we move the site to Bloomsbury and we have it all over again in the attic in a Bloomsbury boarding-house. And that is the variation – the time and place that it all happened. The emphasis is always on the pleasure, the satisfaction, and the sensuality of the episode. And, members of the Jury, when one talks about the book as a whole one reads those particular passages against a background in which you may think sex is dragged in at every conceivable opportunity. The story of this book, apart from those episodes, again you may think, although it is true there is some kind of plot, is little more than padding until we can reach the hut again and the cottage or the undergrowth in the forest. You have that background. You have drawn into it the premarital sexual intercourse that took place between our heroine as a girl and the German boys in Germany where she was studying art.

'The book abounds in bawdy conversation. Even a description of the girl's father, a Royal Academician, has to introduce a description of his legs and loins; and, members of the Jury, even the old nurse who is eventually employed to look after her husband, the heroine's husband, without any point to it whatsoever, without adding anything at all, you may think, to the story, has to have her breasts felt while she is looking after him in his bed. Members of the Jury, not only that type of background, but words – no doubt they will be said to be good old Anglo-Saxon four-letter words, and no doubt they are – appear again and again. These matters are not voiced normally in this Court, but when it forms the whole subject matter of the Prosecution, then, members of the Jury, we cannot avoid voicing them. The word "fuck" or "fucking" occurs no less than thirty times. I have added them up, but I do not guarantee that I have added them all up. "Cunt" fourteen times; "balls" thirteen times; "shit" and "arse" six times apiece; "cock" four times; "piss" three times, and so on. Members of the Jury, it is against that background, as I say, that you have to view those passages.

'Now let us look at the book. You see, the normal Penguin cover on it. Let us open the front cover. There we have a short description: "Lawrence wrote of *Lady Chatterley's Lover* '. . . I always labour at the same thing, to make the sex relation valid and precious instead of shameful. And this novel is the furthest I've gone'." Members of the Jury, you may think that nobody could go much further. "'To me it is beautiful and tender as the naked self . . .' This story of the love between a game-keeper and the wife of a crippled intellectual is therefore one of 'phallic tenderness'" (Members of the Jury, for those of you who have forgotten your Greek, "phallus" means the image of the man's penis) "and is never, in any sense of the word, pornographic. Unfortunately, the critics and censors who bitterly decried the book concentrated their attacks on the language and ignored the tenderness. Lawrence knew that he would be attacked. 'It will bring me only abuse and hatred', he said, and it did. It has taken over thirty years for it to be possible to publish the unmutilated version of the book in this country." Members of the Jury, it is for you in effect to say now whether it has taken only thirty years or whether it will take still longer.'

The Opening Address for the Defence

Gerald Gardiner

'Members of the Jury, you have now heard from my learned friend Mr Griffith-Jones the nature of the case for the Prosecution. He has told you in general terms what this book is about and the grounds on which the Prosecution contend that it is obscene. He has told you it is full of repeated descriptions of sexual intercourse, and so it is. He has told you it is full of large numbers of four-letter words, and so it is. And you may have asked yourselves at once how comes it that reputable publishers should publish, apparently after considerable thought, quite deliberately, an appalling book of the nature which has been described to us.

'So perhaps I should start by telling you something about the defendant company. Because when anybody is charged with any crime their good character, it has been said, is like credit at the bank, something you can draw on in a time of trouble.

'In 1935 there was a man called Lane, in his thirties, who had been in the publishing business, and he thought it would be a good thing if the ordinary people were able to afford to buy good books. The ordinary book was expensive then, as it is expensive now. He himself had not had the advantage of being at a university. He had a passion for books. He left school at the age of 16.

'Of course, people can get books from libraries, but it is not the same thing as having one's own books. Of course, there were those who thought he was mad. They said it's no good giving the working classes good books, they wouldn't understand them if they read them. The next year he formed this company, Penguin Books Limited, to publish good books at the price of ten cigarettes. (The cost of publishing books has now gone up even faster than the cost of cigarettes.) It was 6d.

'He started off with novels and detective stories. Then there were the Penguin Classics, translations from Latin and Greek, masterpieces of literature of other countries. Penguin poetry, Penguin plays, Penguin art, some called Pelicans which were non-fictional: economics, sociology, in fact every subject.

'Whether he was right or wrong in thinking the average person would buy good books if they had the chance is perhaps shown by the fact that since then this company has made and sold 250 – perhaps I might repeat that – 250 million books.

'It was not their intention to seek to publish new books, but substantially to republish, in a form and at a price which the ordinary people could afford to buy, all the great books in our literature. The whole of Shakespeare's works, Shaw (ten volumes of Shaw were published on his ninetieth birthday), and by 1950 they had published four books by D. H. Lawrence. In 1950, that being twenty years after Lawrence's death, they published a further ten of his books, and in 1960, thirty years after his death, they endeavoured to publish the rest, including this book.

'This book has, unfortunately, had a chequered history. It was not published in this country at the time. It would I think be conceded that as the law was thirty years ago it would have been against the law to do so. Of course, there are many books in London now circulating freely which nobody would think ought to be prevented from publication and which have been banned in earlier years – say twenty years ago. This book in English, you will hear, was published on the Continent. No doubt many copies found their way to this country, so it has never been unknown to anyone.

'I shall be calling a great number of witnesses. I think you will find nearly all of them read the unexpurgated edition years ago. The book that Lawrence wrote has never before been published in this country. There has been an expurgated edition and there would have been nothing to stop Penguin Books from publishing an expurgated edition years ago, but they have never thought of doing so. Because, whether they could have made money or not, they have never published a mutilated book.

'The expurgated edition, you will appreciate, is not the book that Lawrence wrote. You can, of course, have an expurgated edition of *Hamlet*, which no doubt has things in it which are, *prima facie*, obscene. You can have an expurgated edition of the *Canterbury Tales*, which would not be the book which Chaucer wrote. They have always refused to publish any work unless it was the work of the author.

'Before this Act the law had three defects which Parliament has now recognized. The first was that the Prosecution could pick out particular passages from a book and say "Just look at those. Don't bother about the rest." Whereas if one is to be fair to an author when one is considering whether a work tends to deprave or corrupt, one must, of course, judge by the whole book. Secondly, the question used to be whether the work had a tendency to deprave or corrupt those whose minds were open to such immoral influences. That at once made everyone think of young people, and referred to nothing but young people. If applied literally it would have meant that our literature would be such as was suitable for a sixteen-year-old schoolgirl. So Parliament got rid of the words about "those whose minds are open to such immoral influences". Thirdly, there was no distinction between pornography and literature. Pornography means literally the writings of prostitutes, but it is now used in a much more general sense, and you may think the best definition is "dirt for dirt's sake" – works which we have all seen and can see on bookstalls, not excepting our Sunday papers. That which is put in for the purpose of selling them has no art, no literature. Mr Justice Stable [in a judgement referred to earlier in the case] said: "I do not suppose there is a decent man or woman in this court who does not wholeheartedly believe that pornography, the filthy bawdy muck that is just filth for filth's sake, ought to be stamped out and suppressed. Such books are not literature. They have got no message; they have got no inspiration; they have got no thought. They have got nothing. They are just filth and ought to be stamped out."'

The Defence Witnesses

Rebecca West examined

'It has been suggested,' said Mr Gardiner, 'that this is a book which sets upon a pedestal promiscuous and adulterous intercourse?' – 'Er, yes,' replied Dame Rebecca. 'It has been suggested, and that on the bare facts is true; but it is not a recommendation of such intercourse. It shows a broken life, and what somebody did with it, but it does not suggest adultery. It could not, because Lawrence was a man who spent all his life working out the problem of how to make a good marriage: he thought a good marriage was perhaps the most important thing in the world.'

'It has been suggested that sex is dragged in at every conceivable opportunity, and that the story is little more than padding. If that was true would it obviously be an attack upon the integrity and honesty of purpose of the writer?' – 'Yes. The idea that the story is padding cannot be true because as a matter of fact the book has that story because it was designed from the first as an allegory. Here was culture that had become sterile and unhelpful to man's deepest needs, and he wanted to have the whole of civilization realizing that it was not living fully enough, that it would be exploited in various ways if it did not try to get down to the springs of its being and live more fully and bring its spiritual gifts into play. The baronet and his impotence are a symbol of the impotent culture of his time; and the love affair with the gamekeeper was a calling, a return of the soul to the more intense life that he felt when people had had a different culture, such as the cultural basis of religious faith.'

'Is Lawrence's message any less valid in today's circumstances than in the circumstances of 1920?' – 'No, I think it has more bearing on them. Since then we have had a war which was due to something that Lawrence feared very much. Lawrence was a very practical and realistic man and he did see that in every country in the world there were vast urban populations who had lost touch with real life, and that they could be taken in any direction. They have been taken in the direction of evil by their obedience to leaders such as Hitler. Lawrence was talking about something quite real. He was not a fanciful writer. He did write about reality. Talking to one, he was governed by the fear that something would happen, and he did want to get back to something which would save us.'

'Is there anything else you would like to say as to the literary merits of the book?' – 'The great literary merit of his book is something that readers accord by reading him in such large numbers, and his critics accord by writing so much about him. But it is not an easy matter to define the literary merit. If you take individual sentences of his, you can find passages which appear to have no literary merit at all; but the same is true of Shakespeare and Wordsworth, who have some terrible lines both in verse and prose, and of Dickens. But if you take Lawrence's books as a whole they are books of great literary merit. If you take all his books together he was a great writer.'

'Don't trouble about these other books,' said Mr Justice Byrne. 'We are only dealing with one. What is the literary merit of this book? I think that is what Mr Gardiner is asking you?' – '*Lady Chatterley's Lover* is full of sentences of which any child could make a fool, because they are badly written. He was a man with no background of formal education in his home. He also had a great defect which mars this book. He had absolutely no sense of humour. A lot of pages in this book are, to my point of view, ludicrous, but I would still say this is a book of undoubted literary merit. After all, a work of art is not an arbitrary thing. A work of art is an analysis of an experience, and a synthesis of the findings of the analysis, that makes life a serious matter and makes the world seem beautiful. And though there are ugly things, though there is this unsuccessful attempt to handle the ugly words, this is still from that standard a good book in my opinion.'

The Bishop of Woolwich examined

'Has the Church,' said Mr Gardiner, 'always had a special interest and a special concern in human relations?' –

'Clearly, that would be one of my chief interests in this whole case, the effect upon human relations and the effect upon Christian judgements and Christian values.'

'What do you say are the ethical merits of the book?' – 'I would not want to be put in a position of arguing this primarily on its ethical merits. Clearly, Lawrence did not have a Christian valuation of sex, and the kind of sexual relationship depicted in the book is not one that I would necessarily regard as ideal, but what I think is clear is that what Lawrence is trying to do is to portray the sex relationship as something essentially sacred. Archbishop William Temple . . .'

Mr Justice Byrne interrupted:

'Before you talk about Archbishop William Temple, he was trying to portray – what?' – 'The sex relation as essentially something sacred. I was quoting Archbishop William Temple. He once said that Christians do not make jokes about sex for the same reason that they do not make jokes about Holy Communion, not because it is sordid, but because it is sacred, and I think Lawrence tried to portray this relation as in a real sense something sacred, as in a real sense an act of holy communion. For him flesh was completely sacramental of spirit. His description of sexual relations cannot be taken out of the context of his whole, to me, quite astonishing sensitivity to the beauty and value of all organic relationships. Some of his descriptions of nature in the book seem to me to be extraordinarily beautiful and delicate and portraying an attitude to the whole organic world of which he saw sex as the culmination, which

I think in no sense anybody could possibly describe as sordid.'

'Would you make any difference', Mr Gardiner asked, 'between the merits from that point of view of the book as it is and those of the book as it would be if the descriptions of sexual intercourse and all four-letter words were expurgated from it?' – 'I think the whole effect of that would be to suggest that what Lawrence was doing was something sordid in putting it before the public, if these things were eliminated. I think that is a false suggestion, and neither in intention nor in effect is this book depraving.'

'It has been suggested that it places upon a pedestal promiscuous and adulterous intercourse.' – 'That seems to me to be a very distorted way of looking at it. It is dealing with sexual relationship, and many books do that. I think it has artistic integrity. It is not dealing with intercourse for its own sake, and it is not dealing with sexual promiscuity. If the Jury read the last two pages, there is a most moving advocacy of chastity and the remark "How can men want wearisomely to philander?", and I think that is Lawrence's whole approach to the subject, and that the effect of this book is against rather than for promiscuity.'

'Have you one son and three daughters?' – 'I have,' said the Bishop; and this concluded his evidence-in-chief.

'I must just point out to you,' said Mr Griffith-Jones, rising to cross-examine after lunch, 'that I don't propose to discuss with you what Lawrence intended. Did you tell us that this book is a valuable work on ethics?' – 'I would say that its value, its positive value, from the ethical point of view is that it does stress the real value and integrity of personal relations; that sex is not just a means of using other people but a means of respect for them.'

'Marriage is another aspect of ethics, is it not?' – 'Certainly.'

'This book doesn't help much in educating anybody into a correct view about that particular aspect of ethics?' – 'Naturally it is not a treatise on marriage. What it does though is, I think, to make it obvious he is not against the marriage relationship. On the contrary, he is concerned with establishing a permanent, genuine, spiritual relationship between persons.'

'Bishop, I don't want to be offensive to you, but you are not here to make speeches,' said Mr Griffith-Jones unexpectedly. 'Just try and answer my question "Yes" or "No", if you can.' 'With respect,' said Mr Gardiner at once, 'the witness *has* answered the question.'

Mr Griffith-Jones went back to his first question. 'Are you asking the Jury to accept that this book is a valuable work on ethics?' – 'It depends on what you mean by a valuable work on ethics.'

'A work of instructional value.' – 'As I said, it doesn't set out to be a treatise on ethics.'

'I am not asking you what it sets out to be; I am asking you to apply your mind to my question and answer it if you can "yes" or "no". Are you suggesting this book is of instructional value upon the subject of ethics?' – 'No, I would not say it was of instructional value upon the subject of ethics.'

'As you read the book,' interposed Mr Justice Byrne, 'does it portray the life of an immoral woman?' – 'It portrays the life of a woman in an immoral relationship, in so far as adultery is an immoral relationship. I would not say it was intended in any way to exalt immorality.'

Mr Gardiner put a few further questions to the Bishop in re-examination. 'Lawrence, of course, was not a Christian, was he?' – 'No.'

'Is this a book which in your view Christians ought to read?' – 'Yes, I think it is. Because I think what Lawrence was trying to do . . .'

This had two consequences: it supplied a banner headline for the evening papers, A BOOK ALL CHRISTIANS SHOULD READ; and it brought Mr Griffith-Jones to his feet again. 'Before you answer that question; if my learned friend keeps putting that form of question I shall keep objecting. That is a matter for the Jury, as to whether the publication of this book is justified.' – 'Justified on the ground of literary or other merits,' said the Judge thoughtfully. And Mr Griffith-Jones added, 'For the public good.' – 'For the public good, yes. I will hear what Mr Gardiner has to say.'

'My Lord,' said Mr Gardiner with a faint air of proprietorship, 'here is a Bishop. The Jury have to consider the question of the public good. Here is an important aspect of public good. It seems strange that the

Prosecution should object to evidence, from a witness of this standing, of his view upon the Christian standpoint.' – 'I think it is really going on to the question the Jury have to answer,' decided the Judge. 'I think he can express his views with regard to the merits of the book from the ethical point of view and so forth, but I think the answer to that last question would really be the very question the Jury might have to answer, assuming they answer the first question in a particular way.' – 'If your Lordship pleases,' Mr Gardiner said, and the Bishop stood down.

Richard Hoggart examined

Then came Mr Richard Hoggart, author of *The Uses of Literacy*, Senior Lecturer in English Literature at Leicester University. He was introduced to the Jury as a man who went from elementary school and grammar school to university and took an English degree. He said that he lectured on D. H. Lawrence to 'the young people under his care'. He was a member of the Albemarle Committee on the Youth Services and of the Pilkington Committee on broadcasting. Mr Hutchinson asked him what he thought about the literary merit of *Lady Chatterley's Lover*. 'I think it is a book of quite exceptional literary merit, probably one of the best twenty novels we have had written in Britain in the last thirty years', said Mr Hoggart.

'It has been said that the two main characters in the

book are little more than bodies which continuously have sexual intercourse together. What would you say to that as a fair summary of this novel in relation to its main characters?' – 'I should think it was a grossly unfair summary. I should think it was based on a misreading of the book.'

'The book has also been described as little more than vicious indulgence in sex and sensuality. In your view is that a valid description of this novel?' – 'I think it is invalid on all three counts. It is not in any sense vicious; it is highly virtuous and if anything, puritanical.'

'Did you say "virtuous and puritanical"?' interrupted Mr Justice Byrne. And Mr Hoggart, who was a self-composed, determined, and unshakeable witness, said that he did. He added that 'indulgence' was not the word for the love passages in the story. 'The sexual encounters, the parts in which we have descriptions of sexual life, are all carefully woven into the psychological relationship, the context of the two people, and the natural flow from this as part of an attempt at explaining their outlet, either physical or spiritual. The third word in the statement is?' And Mr Hutchinson repeated:

'Vicious indulgence in sex and sensuality.' – 'The book obviously includes sensual passages because they are part of the relationship, but certainly not indulgent and certainly not vicious. I thought, taken as a whole, it was a moral book.'

'We know one of the complaints is that it uses four-letter words. What exactly do you mean by saying that, taken as a whole, you think the book is a moral book?' –

'I mean that the overwhelming impression which comes out to me as a careful reader of it is of the enormous reverence which must be paid by one human being to another with whom he is in love and, in particular, the reverence towards one's physical relationships. Physical relationships are not matters in which we use one another like animals. A physical relationship which is not founded in a much closer personal respect is a vicious thing. This spirit seems to me to pervade *Lady Chatterley* throughout, and in this it seems that it is highly moral and not degrading of sex.'

'As far as the young people under your care are concerned, would you think that this was a proper book for them to read?' – 'Viewed purely in the abstract, I would think it proper, if they came to me to ask me if they could read it, to tell them to ask their parents, and probably I should give them a note to their parents asking them if they could read it, but I would not take that responsibility upon myself.'

'You would think that a wise course?' – 'Yes.'

'Have you children of your own?' – 'Yes.'

'By the time you have reached the end of the book, have those two persons, in your view of the reading of it, found some true and real contact, as opposed to all the contacts at the beginning of the book?' – 'Yes, I think the ending of the book has a result which one can hardly find in literature now. He is able to say things in the letter he writes at the end, the very last page, "Now is the time to be chaste, it is so good to be chaste, like a river of cool water in my soul." This is the writing of a pure man. "I love the chastity now that it flows between us. It is like fresh water and rain. How can men want wearisomely to philander," that is, to be promiscuous. This seems to me a resolution which establishes that the book has moved through the whole cycle.'

'It is quite obvious, of course, that this relationship is between two people who in fact are married. Would you say this book advocates – it obviously describes – but would you say it advocates adultery?' – 'I think the book advocates marriage, not adultery. It takes a difficult and distressing human situation which we know exists. A marriage which has gone wrong, which had never started right. It doesn't burke the issue by saying they went on somehow, and this is very much to the point. He could have made this analysis of the realization of the solution through sex by a wife who did not love her husband. He stacked the cards against himself. He was talking about the nature of a true marriage relationship between people. We know there are bound to be occasions in human beings, sometimes for very bad reasons and sometimes for reasons that are unavoidable, when there is friction between our formal state of marriage and the relationship we meet with, the genuine relationship he is talking about. He did not say, if you want to enjoy yourself in sex you should leave your wife or husband, but the thing to do in a marriage was to work hard at every level. When you get up in the morning and cook the breakfast, don't lose your temper with the children. Having gone through all this they will get married. He tells us so; they are waiting for it.'

'In your view is there anything more in this book than, at the end, two people finding a state of satisfactory sexual relationship?' – 'There is not only more in it than that, but one could say – although it sounds paradoxical – one could say the physical sexual side is subordinate. I am sure it was for Lawrence. He said more than once that really he is not interested, not unduly interested, in sexual acts. He is interested in a relationship between people which is in the deepest sense spiritual. This includes a due and proper regard for our sexual and physical side. I believe in this book what he said is, "I must face this problem head on, even at the risk of having people think I am obsessed by sex." But one realizes from this last letter that, between Mellors and Lady Chatterley, there will be periods of extraordinary chasteness; there will be moments of coming together in love which will be all the better because they are not using one another like creatures for enjoyment. It is a kind of sacrament for him.'

'I want to pass now to the four-letter words. You told the Jury yesterday you were educated at an elementary school. Where was it?' – 'Leeds.'

'How did you start your life?' – 'I was born into the working class and I was orphaned at the age of eight and brought up by my grandmother.'

'What is your view as to the genuineness and necessity in this book of the use of these four-letter words in the mouth of Mellors?' – 'They seem to me totally characteristic of many people, and I would like to say not only working-class people, because that would be wrong. They are used, or seem to me to be used, very freely indeed, far more freely than many of us know. Fifty yards from this Court this morning I heard a man say "fuck" three times as he passed me. He was speaking to himself and he said "fuck it, fuck it, fuck it" as he went past. If you have worked on a building site, as I have, you will find they recur over and over again. The man I heard this morning and the men on building sites use the words as words of contempt, and one of the things Lawrence found most worrying was that the word for this important relationship had become a word of vile abuse. So one would say "fuck you" to a man, although the thing has totally lost its meaning; it has become simply derision, and in this sense he wanted to re-establish the meaning of it, the proper use of it.'

'What do you say about the use of these words as they have been used in this book?' – 'The first effect, when I first read it, was some shock, because they don't go into polite literature normally. Then as one read further on one found the words lost that shock. They were being progressively purified as they were used. We have no word in English for this act which is not either a long abstraction or an evasive euphemism, and we are constantly running away from it, or dissolving into dots, at a passage like that. He wanted us to say "This is what one does. In a simple, ordinary way, one fucks", with no sniggering or dirt.'

*

Mr Griffith-Jones, who now rose to cross-examine, had been wondering whether Mr Hoggart belonged to 'a body of opinion' that was opposed to all prosecutions for obscenity. 'Certainly not,' said Mr Hoggart. 'I think the question of freedom of expression is a most involved and complicated one.'

Mr Griffith-Jones then mounted his main attack on Mr Hoggart's view of the book. 'Do you regard the real importance of this book as that part which does not consist in the descriptions of sexual intercourse?' – 'I regard the importance of the book as not separable from the whole book, including the parts about sexual intercourse.'

'I should have thought that was a question which was capable of a simple answer,' said Mr Griffith-Jones, looking round the Court. 'Would you regard the real importance of this book as being that part of it which is not contained in the descriptions of sexual intercourse?' – 'No', said Mr Hoggart firmly and patiently.

'You described this book as highly virtuous, if not puritanical. Please do not think that I am suggesting it with any bad faith against you. That is your genuine and considered view, is it?' – 'Yes.'

'I thought I had lived my life under a misapprehension as to the meaning of the word "puritanical". Will you help me?' Mr Hoggart took this as a genuine cry for help. 'Yes,' he said, 'many people do live their lives under a misapprehension of the meaning of the word "puritanical". This is the way in which language decays. In England today and for a long time the word "puritanical" has been extended to mean somebody who is against anything which is pleasurable, particularly sex. The proper meaning of it, to a literary man or to a linguist, is somebody who belongs to the tradition of British puritanism generally, and the distinguishing feature of that is an intense sense of responsibility for one's conscience. In this sense this book is puritanical.'

'I am obliged for that lecture upon it. I want to see a little more precisely what you describe as "puritanical". Will you look at page 30? On page 30 there is a description of the second "bout", if I may again borrow a word, with the man Michaelis. Do you see towards the bottom of the page: "He roused in the woman a wild sort of compassion and yearning, and a wild, craving physical desire. The physical desire he did not satisfy in her; he was always come and finished so quickly, then shrinking down on her breast, and recovering somewhat his effrontery while she lay dazed, disappointed, lost. But then she soon learnt to hold him, to keep him there inside her when his crisis was over. And there he was generous and curiously potent; he stayed firm inside her, giving to her, while she was active . . . wildly, passionately active, coming to her own crisis. And as he felt the frenzy of her achieving her own orgasmic satisfaction from his hard, erect passivity, he had a curious sense of pride and satisfaction. 'Ah, how good!' she whispered tremulously, and she became quite still, clinging to him. And he lay there in his own isolation, but somehow proud." Is that a passage which you describe as puritanical?' – 'Yes, puritanical, and poignant, and tender, and moving, and sad, about two people who have no proper relationship.'

E. M. Forster examined

'I think,' said Mr Hutchinson, 'you knew D. H. Lawrence quite well?' – 'Yes, I saw a good deal of him in 1915. That was the time when I saw him most, but we kept in touch.'

'Would you tell us where you would place him as a novelist and a writer in literature?' – 'In all the literature of the day, do you mean; in all contemporary literature?' – 'Yes?' – 'I should place him enormously high. When one comes to the upper ten novels then one has to begin to think a little of the order, but compared with all novels which come out, the novels he wrote dominate terrifically.'

'When he died I think you described him as the greatest imaginative novelist of your generation?' – 'Yes, I would still hold to it.'

'You have read *Lady Chatterley's Lover*?' – 'Yes.'

'Judging it in the same way, what would you say as to its literary merit?' – 'Judging it in the same way, I should say that it had very high literary merit. It is, perhaps I might add, not the novel of Lawrence which I most admire. That would be *Sons and Lovers*, I think.'

'Lawrence has been described as forming part of the great Puritan stream of writers in this country. Have you any comment to make on that?' – 'I think the description is a correct one, though I understand that at first people would think it paradoxical. But when I was thinking over this matter beforehand, I considered his relationship to Bunyan. They both were preachers. They both believed intensely in what they preached. I would say, if I may speak of antecedents, of great names, Bunyan on the one hand and Blake on the other, Lawrence too had this passionate opinion of the world and what it ought to be, but is not.'

'Is that founded not only on what he has written but what you knew of him?' – 'Yes. Well . . .'

'Thank you very much,' said Mr Hutchinson, and sat down.

'Did you want to add something?' asked the Judge. – 'I was only qualifying it a little, because I did not discuss these questions with Lawrence personally, but there is nothing in what I knew of him which would contradict what I said.'

Norman St John-Stevas examined

Mr Hutchinson asked him a double-barrelled question about the book's literary *and* moral value. 'Well,' said Mr St John-Stevas, 'as to literary merit, I would say it was a book of high literary merit. I would not say it was the best book Lawrence ever wrote, but I think it is a very well-written book and is a contribution of consid-erable value to English literature. On the moral ques-tion, it does seem to me that this is undoubtedly a

moral book. It is not, of course, and I am not suggesting I think it is, a book that puts forward an orthodox
Christian view, or an orthodox Roman Catholic view –
and this is not surprising because Lawrence was not a
Christian or a Catholic. I have formed the view, after a
careful reading of the book, that Lawrence is essentially a writer in the Catholic tradition. By "within the
Catholic tradition" I mean the tradition which regards
the sexual instinct as good in itself. It is implanted in
man by God, and it is one of his greatest gifts; we
should always be grateful for this. And I think that this
tradition has been opposed since the Reformation era
when sex was regarded as something essentially evil.
So I would have no hesitation in saying that every
Catholic priest and every Catholic would profit by reading this book, because really they have an aim in
common, which is this, to rid the sexual instinct, the
sexual act, of any taint of false shame.' (Mr St John-
Stevas later stressed that he was not speaking officially
on behalf of his Church.)

'Do you find that consistent with the tenets of your
own faith?' – 'I certainly find it quite consistent with my
own faith; and I would add this: I would put Lawrence
amongst the great literary moralists of our own English
literature, a man who was essentially trying to purge
and to cleanse and to reform, and I have been horrified
at the representations in some papers which have been
calling him a vicious man – papers which I think he
would not have deigned himself to read.'

'During the time which you spent in studying and in

research to write the book which I have mentioned, called *Obscenity and the Law*, did you have to read a very large number of books in relation to that matter?' – 'I did.'

'And I think in fact you acted as a legal adviser to the Committee which was originally set up to sponsor the new Bill which eventually became this Act of Parliament?' – 'Yes.'

'In view of your study of those books in relation to the matter of *Obscenity and the Law*, I want to ask you about the literary merit of this book as compared to the literary merit of the large number of books which you have had to study and read.'

'My Lord,' objected Mr Griffith-Jones, 'again I do not know whether this is admissible even on literary merit. This book has to be judged as a book and it may be judged with other books, generally speaking, but can it be permissible to judge this book with other books which are or may be obscene?' – 'Well, we did discuss this the other day,' said the Judge, 'and I have ruled, rightly or wrongly, that in fact, as far as literary merit is concerned, this book could be compared with other books.'

'Your Lordship did, but it was not confined to a comparison with other books which might be said to be of an obscene nature.' – 'No.'

'That is what I understood this to lead to.' – 'I don't know that I did extract that meaning. Mr Hutchinson, you can help me about this.'

'My Lord, the last thing I want to do,' said Mr

Hutchinson, 'is to put a question which is capable of two meanings.' – 'What I did say,' answered the Judge, 'was that there must be no comparison upon any basis of obscenity, and I said there *could* be a comparison upon the basis of literary merit.' – 'Yes, my Lord.' – 'As long as you confine yourself within "literary merit" you are within the ruling which, rightly or wrongly, I have laid down; but if you go outside that, then you will be outside the ruling.'

'I had hoped the question I put was quite clearly within that ruling.' – 'I am sure you will do your best to keep within the limits.'

'Yes, my Lord', promised Mr Hutchinson. 'Mr Stevas, I am sure, being a lawyer yourself, you understand the position and what you may say and what you may not say as regards the law, and restricting this matter entirely to literary merit?' – 'Yes.'

'Have you any observation to make?' – 'I would say I am only an academic lawyer and therefore my knowledge of the law of evidence is not a very deep one. This is just to excuse myself in case I go over the bounds of my Lord's permission.'

'We will stop you if you do,' said Mr Justice Byrne with a monitory smile. – 'But I have certainly read a great many books of a pornographic and obscene nature in connexion with this study, and my judgement is, with regard to literary merit, that, of course, *Lady Chatterley's Lover* has nothing in common with those books. And I would use "literary merit" there not only in the sense of the language but – I do not think this can be separated – the theme and method and the underlying morality of the book. These books which I have studied have nothing to be said for them at all, and I find it difficult to make a comparison between them and *Lady Chatterley's Lover* because the gulf between them is so great.'

Sir Allen Lane examined

'When you first founded the firm,' said Mr Hutchinson, 'what was the idea you had in your mind?' – 'The idea I had was, I had been in publishing for some fifteen years and I felt that although we were publishing extremely good books we were not reaching the market that I thought existed for good books. I thought perhaps price might have something to do with it, or the form in which the books were produced might; and my idea was to produce a book which would sell at the price of ten cigarettes, which would give no excuse for anybody not being able to buy it, and would be the type of book which they would get if they had gone on to further education. For people like myself who left school and started work when they were 16 it would be another form of education.'

'I think you have used the phrase that you wanted to make Penguin a University Press in paper backs.' – 'Yes, I have used the term.'

'Do you only publish works of great literature or do you publish other books or works of a high standard?'

– 'When we started we only published fiction and biographies and travel and detective fiction, but after a couple of years we realized there was a very great field outside those subjects, and that is when we started Pelicans, which we devoted to the arts and sciences.'

'Now, I think in 1952 you were knighted for your services to literature.' – 'Yes.'

'Would you tell us, Sir Allen, what number of titles have you published and about how many copies of books have you sold?' – 'We have published 3,500 titles and our sales are just on 250 million.'

'What were the considerations, as far as you were concerned, which led you to include *Lady Chatterley* among the other Lawrence novels which had not up to that date been published?' – 'What we hoped to do this year was to round off the collection of D. H. Lawrence which we had started in 1950, and we felt *Lady Chatterley* was a book which it was essential should be included if we were in fact going to round off this group.'

'You realized, of course, that it had been a controversial book. In your view did it have high literary merit?' – 'Yes, certainly.'

'Were there any other considerations you took into account in making that decision?' – 'As I think has been said already, we had considered doing this in 1950, and we had not published it for the reason that we wouldn't have been in the position we are in today to defend it; and with reluctance we decided not to publish it. We considered publishing the expurgated version and would not do it. This year, the fact that the new Act was now on the Statute Book and that there had been a trial in America decided us this was a book we should now do.'

'If in fact you had published it in an expurgated form in 1950, as far as sales were concerned, would you have printed an equivalent number on your first printing?' – 'Oh yes, most certainly. We know what the sales are of the American edition, and they have been on sale I should think for at least ten years and we would have known what to expect.'

'Why in fact did you take the view that you should not publish an expurgated edition?' – 'Because it is against our principle. We would not publish a book in an emasculated form. We would only publish it if we were doing what we stated we were doing, that is selling the book as written by the author.'

Cecil Day Lewis examined

Mr Griffith-Jones cross-examined at some length. 'It is really recommending a right and full relationship between a man and a woman who are virtually unknown to one another, is it not?' – 'They are unknown to one another at the beginning of their relationship, yes.'

'And even at the end they have had virtually no conversation about any topic at all, have they, except sexual intercourse?' – 'No, I would not agree with that.'

'Well, just take the book, would you, sir. Tell me if there is anything in that book which indicates, for example, conversation between the two which is about anything other than sexual intercourse?' – 'There is a great deal of conversation, I would say, between Lady Chatterley and the gamekeeper which is not a conversation about the sexual side of love alone.'

'Well, we won't occupy too long a time. What else did they know of one another? Let me preface it by saying that of course, he tells her about his early love affairs and unsatisfactory sexual intercourse with other women, but, apart from that, what does he tell her about himself?' – 'He tells her about his time in the Army in India as an officer, for instance.'

'Well, that doesn't take her very far in getting to know this man. What else?' – 'I can remember nothing else.'

'And what did she tell him of herself?' – 'She told him about her life with her husband.' – 'Did she?' – 'I think so.'

'Did she? Can you point to any passage where she tells Mellors about her life with her husband?' – 'No, I can't point to it now without looking at the book again.'

'You see, this book is put forward as a tender book, and a book teaching the lesson of true tenderness and understanding, fulfilment and happiness. Is it possible that any two human beings can really love one another when they have said practically not a word to one another about any subject at all except copulation?' – 'Yes, because we cannot assume that the dialogue in the novel is the only conversation between them.'

'The only occasions when they have any opportunity of any conversation is either just before, during, or immediately after the act of copulation. Those are the only occasions, in the circumstances, when any conversation can occur, are they not?' – 'That is so, yes. That is because . . .' But Mr Day Lewis was not allowed to say why it was so.

'Apart from meeting him in the park, I think, when she is out with her husband, can you point to any other occasion when these two people meet, other than when they have copulation?' – 'No. After their first meetings they do in fact copulate on each occasion. They are lovers and it seems to be perfectly natural they should.' – '"Perfectly natural"?' (incredulously.) – 'Yes.'

'"Perfectly natural" that Lady Chatterley should run off to the hut in the forest on every occasion to copulate with her husband's gamekeeper? Not "perfectly natural", sir!' – 'Yes; it is in her nature.'

'It is in her nature because she is an oversexed and adulterous woman; that is why it is in her nature, is it not?' – 'No, I entirely disagree.' – 'Why?' – 'I think it is in her nature because she is an averagely sexed woman, I would say. We have no particular evidence about her one way or the other, but she is a lonely woman who is not getting the affection and love that she needs and her nature sends her to the man who can give it to her.'

The Closing Speech for the Defence

'May I remind you, briefly, of what the witnesses you have heard have said. First of all, as to the author. Now, this is obviously of great importance when one is considering relative questions of literary merit. Obviously, if there were a prosecution for publishing Chaucer's *Canterbury Tales*, the first thing which the Defence would want to do would be to explain to the Jury in some detail Chaucer's standing in the history of English literature. It might be difficult to deny that some of the tales are obscene, but that obviously would be their defence. Now, Lawrence, you see, has been dead for thirty years. He was a highly controversial figure in his lifetime, and it may not be at all easy to judge. Indeed, any survey of the history of art and literature in this country makes it plain, does it not, that in the past we have not found it easy to judge the true merits of a highly controversial figure while he is living? But Lawrence has now been dead thirty years. There are apparently about 800 books all over the world written about him, and people just don't go on reading all the novels of a particular author long after his death unless in fact they are good literature. That really is the test, is it not, when a man has been dead for that length of time?

'There has been talk, although the Prosecution have

not put it in, of an expurgated edition. It has been suggested that it would be much better if there was a whole lot of asterisks. On the *un*expurgated edition, Professor Muir was asked "What do you take to be the theme of the unexpurgated edition?", and he said, "I should say the redemption of the individual, and hence of society, by what Lawrence calls 'reciprocity of tenderness', and that is why I feel that the expurgated edition is a travesty of the original and ought never to have been published." Mr Connell, when sent an expurgated edition for review, said he found it "(a) trivial, (b) furtive, (c) obscene".

'It was then suggested that perhaps it would have been nice to have published, instead of this book, what has been called the first version, which, apparently many years after Lawrence's death, was published (I think in America) under the title *The First Lady Chatterley*. It is not a "version", properly called, at all. I suppose it might be interesting to students of literature to see the first rough draft of *Sons and Lovers* so as to see how Lawrence's mind progressed and how he carried out his creative function, but the first draft of any of his books is not really a "version" at all; it is merely what he says it was, a first rough draft. It is said that to publish that would be quite all right because that version contains the letters "f . . k" and "c . . t". Have we really descended to this? Are we so frightened of words that while it is perfectly all right to publish a book with "f . . k" it is all wrong to publish a book with the word in its full form? This would in fact have destroyed the whole purpose with which Lawrence was using the words. People in real life do not say "f . . k". After all, these words have been part of spoken English for hundreds and hundreds of years. They are apparently known not only to boys but also to girls at school age.

'When it is said that this is a book about adultery, one wonders how there can be things which people do not see. I suppose it is possible that somewhere there might be a mind which would describe *Antony and Cleopatra* as "a tale about adultery". Antony had a wife in Rome, and I suppose there might be a mind somewhere which would describe this play of Shakespeare's as "the story of a sex-starved man copulating with an Egyptian queen", a parallel with the way this book has been put before you on behalf of the Prosecution. Thus there are minds which are unable to see beauty where it exists, and doubt the integrity of purpose in an author where it is obvious.

'I must deal with what no doubt will be a point sought to be made by the Prosecution. "This is in a book published at 3s. 6d. It will be available to the general public." Of course, that is perfectly true and perfectly obvious. It may well be said that everybody will rush to buy it. You may well think *that* is perfectly true and perfectly obvious, because it happens in every case. Whether it is *The Philanderer* or any other book which is wrongly prosecuted, inevitably people go and buy it. It would be idle to deny it. But whose fault is that? It is always the fact that there has been a wrong prosecution of a book that leads a large number of people to buy it. What was said on this aspect of the case was this. I am most anxious not to do my learned friend any injustice, and so may I quote exactly what he said? He invited you to consider this question after you had read it. "Is it a book that you would even wish your wife or your servants to read?" I cannot help thinking that this was, consciously or unconsciously, an echo from an observation which had fallen from the Bench in an earlier case: "It would never do to let members of the working class read this." I do not want to upset the Prosecution by suggesting that there are a certain number of people nowadays who as a matter of fact don't *have* servants. But of course that whole attitude is one which Penguin Books was formed to fight against, which they always have fought against, and which they will go on fighting against – the attitude that it is all right to publish a special edition at five or ten guineas so that people who are less well off cannot read what other people read. Isn't everybody, whether earning £10 a week or £20 a week, equally interested in the society in which we live, in the problems of human relationships including sexual relationships? In view of the reference made to wives, aren't women equally interested in human relations, including sexual relationships?

'The book has to be judged as a whole, in relation to the general public as a whole, and not to some particular section of the public. You see, there are students of literature in all walks of life, and the sale of 250 million books shows, does it not, that Mr Lane (as he then was) was right in thinking that there are. If it is right that this book should be read, it should be available to the man who is working in the factory or to the teacher who is working in the school. It is rather extraordinary on the face of it, is it not, that, when a visiting professor goes from this country to other countries to lecture on Lawrence, he is not supposed, really, to know anything about this book at all.

'Nothing, members of the Jury, will ever prevent young people from looking up certain words in the dictionary, or Shakespeare, or the Old Testament, and as long as there are medical books in the secondhand bookshops, some young people who may look at a particular diagram may not be solely influenced by a desire for medical education. We do not say for that reason that medical books should not be sold. Society cannot fix its standards by what is suitable for a young person of 14.

'My submission is that this book would not deprave or corrupt anyone in real life, young people included; with deference to my friend I should add, not even your wives or servants.

'In my submission the decision of the Board of Penguin Books to include this book in the publication of Lawrence's seven remaining novels which they had not already published, a decision taken responsibly and after taking into account the fact that this is, after all, Lawrence's own country, was a right decision. Lawrence lived and died suffering from a public opinion, caused by the banning of this book, that he had written a piece of pornography called *Lady Chatterley's Lover*, and if this case has done nothing else it has for the first time enabled this book to be dragged out into the light of day so that we can see what it really is, and so that those who are qualified to judge can express their opinion about it. As you have seen in the witness box, those who have been able to read it didn't think that it was anything like the public reputation which it has always had. But because it was banned, students of literature among the general public had had no opportunity of judging for themselves. The slur was never justified. All the time, this book was the passionately sincere book of a moralist in the puritan tradition, who believed he had a message for us and the society in which we live, whether we agree with this message or not. Is it not time that we rescued Lawrence's name from the quite unjust reputation which, because of this book, it has always had, and allowed our people, his people, to judge for themselves its high purpose? Members of the Jury, I leave Lawrence's reputation, and the reputation of Penguin Books, with confidence in your hands.'

The Closing Speech for the Prosecution

'Members of the Jury, there must be standards, must there not – I say this in all seriousness, and no doubt it is a matter which you will consider as serious – which we are to maintain, some standards of morality, some standards of language and conversation, some standards of conduct which are essential to the well-being of our society. There must be, must there not, instilled in all of us, and at the earliest possible age, standards of respect, respect for the conventions of society, for the kind of conduct of which society approves, respect for other people's feeling, respect, you may think too, for the intimacy, the privacy, of relations between people. There must be instilled in all of us, must there not, standards of restraint. And when one sees what is happening today and has been happening, perhaps all the more since the war, restraint becomes all the more essential, does it not, in the education of the youth of our country, and an understanding that restraint is essential.

'As I say, one has only got to read one's daily papers to see the kind of thing [sexual offences] that is happening, and it is all that type of offence, it is all through lack of standards, lack of restraint, lack of discipline – mental, moral discipline. And why? It is because, is it not, of the lack of discipline imposed upon so many of

the younger generation and the influences to which they
are open: the Sunday papers, it may be, as Mr Gardiner
has already suggested, the cinema, it may be, and,
members of the Jury, literature, it may be. How necessary, therefore, it is to bear in mind these considerations
when the decision which you have to take is whether
or not a book of this kind, this book in particular, has
a tendency to deprave and corrupt.

'Members of the Jury, my learned friend has anticipated – as I certainly had anticipated that he would
anticipate – the comments, or some of the comments,
that I was going to make to you, or rather the argu-
ments that I was going to put before you. It is perfectly
true that I am going to urge upon you that it is *you* who
have to decide this case; it is not the various witnesses
whose views you have heard; it is you, and you alone.
You may think – I do not say this in any sense as criti-
cism, for perhaps a little more latitude, and quite rightly
so, is allowed to the Defence than the Prosecution in
all criminal cases – that while witnesses are called as
experts to give their views upon the literary merits and
the sociological merits and the educational merits, no
effort has been spared to impress upon you what also
is in fact the view they take as to whether this book is
obscene or not.

'Whom have we had? Bishops, prebendaries, other
clergymen, the Master of the Temple, schoolteachers
and a fashion page editor, a young girl who has just
started her first novel, all under the guise of literary
experts or sociological experts or educational experts;

and there has not been one that has not been asked whether he has got children.' (In fact, Mr Gardiner had been rather more discriminating than this.) 'What possible relevance, members of the Jury, has that question, unless it be to suggest that, since he is there giving this evidence, having children indicates that he does not think there is anything wrong in the book? "Are you a Roman Catholic?" or "Are you a Presbyterian?" What possible relevance, I ask you? What possible relevance unless it be to ram down your throats that here again is a Presbyterian who does not, apparently, think that this book is obscene? And then, to one of them, "Would you feel any embarrassment in discussing this book in your class?" That, under the guise of educational value! Members of the Jury, you will not be brow-beaten by evidence given by these people upon this question, in effect given as to what they think of this book on the question of whether it is obscene or not. You will judge this as ordinary men and women, with your feet, I trust, firmly planted upon the ground.

'And I do say to you – as my learned friend anticipated that I would – I do say to you, are these views that you have heard from these most eminent and academic ladies and gentlemen, are they really of such value as the views which you (perhaps, if I may say so, without the eminence and without the academic learning that they possess) hold and can see from the ordinary life in which you live?

'Members of the Jury, what is said of this book by these witnesses and by the Defence as a whole? It is said to be in support of marriage. If you accept that, if you think that that is a realistic view of this book, so be it, members of the Jury. Then it is not obscene and I suppose its publication will be justified on educational grounds, or perhaps religious grounds, I know not. But I do not seek to draw fun simply for the fun of drawing fun at their expense by such comments as I make, because let it not be thought for one moment that I question their absolute integrity; I do not. But I do suggest that they have got what in Scotland I think is said to be a bee in their bonnet about this matter, and indeed, when one sees and hears some of them launching themselves at the first opportunity, with the first question that is asked of them, into a sermon or a lecture, according to their vocations in this world, with apostolic fervour, as they did, one cannot help feeling that, sincerely and honestly as they feel, they feel in such a way that common sense perhaps has gone by the board. You have this reverend gentleman regarding this book as a most impressive statement of the Christian view of marriage. Well, there it is.

'It is said that this book condemns promiscuity. Does it? We have dealt with this matter in cross-examination. He said I have not cross-examined everybody. You may feel thankful I have not repeated the points I had to make by putting them to everybody who suggested that this book did not condone promiscuity. But it does, doesn't it? The earlier sexual experiences of both parties, then Michaelis, then Mellors – it is said that this is only showing how perfect sexual intercourse can lead to ultimate happiness. Members of the Jury, the short answer to that view of the matter is this, which I think I put to one witness: what is there in this book to suggest that if the sexual intercourse between Lady Chatterley and Mellors had not eventually turned out to be successful she would not have gone on and on and on elsewhere until she did find it? Indeed it follows, does it not, from what is said to be the main theme of the book – the search and the importance of finding somebody with whom you can have satisfactory sexual intercourse – that until you do find that person you go on looking for him, married or unmarried?

'It was put forward during the course of the evidence, when we had the Bishop of Woolwich here, that this was a book of ethical value! The bishop himself, however, knocked that argument upon the head when he said, "I would not say it was of instructional value upon the subject of ethics." Members of the Jury, I do not suppose that there will be any of you who will disagree with him upon that point.

'"Treatment of sex on a holy basis", said Mrs Russell' (Miss Dilys Powell). 'Can *that* be a realistic view? Is *that* the kind of way in which the young boys and men leaving school, thousands of them, tens of thousands every year, I suppose, leaving school at the age of 15, going into their first jobs this last September, is *that* how they are going to read this book – as a treatment of sex on a holy basis – or is it wholly unrealistic to think that they are?

'Then the bishop again – to return to him – goes one

better than Mrs Russell. "Something sacred," he said, "in a real sense as an act of holy communion." Do you think that that is how the girls working in the factory are going to read this book – as something sacred, in a real sense as an act of holy communion – or does it put my Lord Bishop, with all respect to him, wholly out of touch with a very large percentage of the number of people who are going to buy this book at 3s. 6d.?

'"A book of moral purpose", said the Rev. Mr Hopkinson. What moral purpose do you read into this book, I wonder? What moral purpose do you think that all the young people who are going to read this book are going to see in it?

'"An antidote", said Mr Hemming, the psychologist. Let me quote: "It is an antidote, a positive antidote to the shallow, superficial values of sex which are widely current today and which are now corrupting the attitude of young people towards sex." I do not know – let us be serious – but as I say, no doubt it was honest. But *can* it be said that this book offers "an antidote to the shallow and superficial values of sex which are widely current today and corrupting the attitude of young people"?

'Members of the Jury, may I say a few words about the defence? The real defence, as I understand it (although I don't know that I am justified in saying that because it has been said equally strongly that it is not obscene) is the justification. Its literary merit, its educational merit, and its sociological merit, with possibly ethics thrown in. You see, you have to ask yourselves here, if you come to the conclusion that there *is* a tendency to deprave and corrupt: what is the justification? What good, what public good, is being done by this book to offset, to outweigh, the harm? It is said that the literary merit depends not only upon the actual writing of the book, but quite naturally upon its theme, and we have heard a great deal of evidence about the author's intention. I submit to you again, the author's intention is irrelevant as such; it only becomes relevant as it shows itself through this book.

'Its themes are threefold, as they are put before you: the need for perfect sexual relationships, to be put under the heading of "tenderness"; secondly, that sex should be discussed without shame; and, thirdly, a treatise on the effects, the harmful effects, of the industrialization of the country. One can discount the third because one can almost add up the number of words which are devoted to that particular theme. What about tenderness? is that a theme which it is in the public good to read as expressed in this book? I will tell you how it is expressed in this book, in the words of the book itself: "Tenderness, really – cunt tenderness. Sex is really the closest touch of all. Cunt tenderness." That is the tenderness that this book is advocating through the mouth of one of its chief characters. And again may I quote from my note: "I believe in something" – this is Mellors speaking – "I believe in being warm-hearted. I believe especially in being warm-hearted in love. I believe that if men could fuck with warm hearts and women took it warm-heartedly, everything would come all right." That is put before you as a theme which justifies this book for the public good, the theme advocating to the young of this country who are going to read the book. "Fuck warmheartedly and everything will come all right." Does it justify it?

'Members of the Jury, let me in conclusion come back to the summing-up of Mr Justice Stable, upon which Mr Gardiner has so much relied in this case: "It is the business of the parents and teachers," he said, "and the environment of society to see, so far as possible, that those ideas" – he is talking about the adolescent ideas of young people – "that those ideas are wisely and naturally directed to the fulfilment of a balanced life." Are the ideas, the theme, the language which this book contains directed to the fulfilment of a balanced life? Are authors exempt from those obligations which lie upon society – because books surely are as much a part of the environment of society as anything else, books which are now being read by everybody? Just let us see. I ask your forgiveness, if it be necessary, for referring to just two other passages in the book because it may have been noticed that in my learned friend's address to you the one thing which he never referred you to at all was the contents of this book; and, after all, it is this book that you are trying and it is this book which constitutes the evidence upon which I rely.

'Would you look at page 258. It is a passage which I have not – and I do not think anybody has – referred to during the course of cross-examination, or indeed at any time during this trial. It is that passage which describes what is called the "night of sensual passion".

'"It was a night of sensual passion, in which she was a little startled and almost unwilling: yet it pierced again with piercing thrills of sensuality, different, sharper, more terrible than the thrills of tenderness, but, at the moment, more desirable. Though a little frightened, she let him have his way . . ." Not very easy, sometimes, not very easy, you know, to know what in fact he is driving at in that passage.' This unexpected and totally unheralded innuendo visibly shocked some members of the Jury. '"Though a little frightened, she let him have his way, and the reckless, shameless sensuality shook her to her foundations, stripped her to the very last, and made a different woman of her. It was not really love. It was not voluptuousness. It was sensuality sharp and searing as fire, burning the soul to tinder." I don't know: is this stuff having a good influence on the young reader? "Burning out the shames, the deepest, oldest shames, in the most secret places. It cost her an effort to let him have his way and his will of her." One wonders why, with all the experiences that had gone before!

'Members of the Jury, this book has been likened to *Antony and Cleopatra*. Is it really possible to compare the two? Is it possible to bracket them in the same way, as literature? Is it possible to compare the difference in the effect that the one will have and the other will have?

'Let all these witnesses hold their views, and hold them sincerely, as they no doubt do. It is not they who are deciding this case. Parliament has said that you, twelve men and women of the community, the ordinary community if you will forgive me for saying so, the ordinary run of life, must decide, just in the same way as twelve men and women decide all the cases in this Court – not the so-called experts, not the experts on anything. I ask you to bring to bear upon this matter your knowledge of the world and of the life which the average person leads. I respectfully submit to you that the effect upon that average person must be to deprave and corrupt, must be to lower the general standards of thought, conduct, and decency, and must be the very opposite to encouraging that restraint in sexual matters which is so all-important at the present time.

'I submit to you further that there is nothing in this document which is of such great value as literature, from an educational point of view, or from a sociological point of view, nothing in this book of such value, as can justify its publication for the public good.'

The Verdict

'Members of the Jury,' said the Clerk, 'are you agreed upon your verdict?' The usher motioned to the foreman to stand up. 'We are,' said the foreman, standing up.

'Do you find that Penguin Books Ltd are guilty or not guilty of publishing an obscene article?' – 'NOT GUILTY,' said the foreman.

POCKET PENGUINS

POCKET PENGUINS